D1090973

WHAT IS THE STRUCTURE OF AN ANIMAL?

LOUISE SPILSBURY

Britannica
Educational Publishing

IN ASSOCIATION WITH

ROSEN
EDUCATIONAL SERVICES

Published in 2014 by Britannica Educational Publishing (a trademark of Encyclopædia Britannica, Inc.) in association with The Rosen Publishing Group, Inc.
29 East 21st Street, New York, NY 10010

Distributed exclusively by Rosen Publishing.
To see additional Britannica Educational Publishing titles, go to rosenpublishing.com

First Edition

Britannica Educational Publishing
J.E. Luebering: Director, Core Reference Group
Anthony L. Green: Editor, Compton's by Britannica

Rosen Publishing
Hope Lourie Killcoyne: Executive Editor
Nelson Sá: Art Director

Library of Congress Cataloging-in-Publication Data

Spilsbury, Louise, author.
What is the structure of an animal?/Louise Spilsbury. — First edition.
    pages cm. — (Let's find out. Life science)
Audience: Grades 3 to 6.
Includes bibliographical references and index.
ISBN 978-1-62275-246-1 (library binding) — ISBN 978-1-62275-249-2 (pbk.) — ISBN 978-1-62275-250-8 (6-pack)
1. Animals—Juvenile literature. 2. Anatomy—Juvenile literature. 3. Physiology—Juvenile literature. I. Title.
SF768.S65 2014
591—dc23
2013026799

Manufactured in the United States of America.

CONTENTS

What Is an Animal?

Animals are as different as a starfish and an ostrich, a tuna and a gibbon. Yet, they are alike because they have features in common. Animals are living things that eat food, move, and sense and react to the world around them.

▶▶ **Animals need to get food to survive. Some animals do this by killing other animals.**

We can tell different types of animal apart by looking at the structure of their bodies. Most animals have no backbone. These are invertebrates. Some animals, including people, have backbones. They are vertebrates.

Many structural features help animals survive. These are called adaptations. For example, bats have wings to fly, so they can find food and escape danger.

Beak

THINK ABOUT IT
A shark looks very different from a tree. What are the ways animals are different from plants?

▶▶ A bird's beak is an adaptation to help it catch food.

5

Worms

Worms are soft, long invertebrates. Some worms are fat, some are very thin, like threads. Others are flat, like ribbons. Some worms are so tiny you can hardly see them, while others grow up to 100 feet (30 m) long! Worms are found all over the world, except where the ground is frozen or too dry for them to survive there.

▶▶ **Some flatworms that live in the sea are brightly colored.**

THINK ABOUT IT
Earthworms have tiny spikes along their bodies. How do you think these structures help them move underground?

Earthworms live and feed in rich, damp soil.

Earthworms have mouths at one end of their bodies, which take in soil as they wriggle through it. They sift out food from the soil, and dump the waste dirt.

Some worms feed off other animals. Tapeworms live inside the guts of other animals, and take in food from the guts through the walls of their bodies.

MOLLUSKS

Mollusks are invertebrates, such as snails and squid. They usually have shells that protect their soft bodies. Mollusks have a distinct head and a single, muscular foot, which they use to move around. A snail glides along on its slimy foot. An octopus's foot is shaped into eight tentacles, which it uses to crawl over the sea floor.

The giant clam is the biggest mollusk with a shell. It can grow to more than 54 inches (137 cm) and can live up to 40 years!

Clams, mussels, and scallops have shells made up of two pieces, which open and close. They suck water into the shells and strain out bits of food. Squid and octopuses are mollusks without a shell.

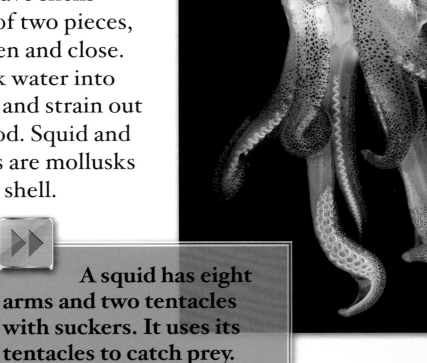

A squid has eight arms and two tentacles with suckers. It uses its tentacles to catch prey.

THINK ABOUT IT
When the tide goes out on seashores, clams cling to rocks and mussels clamp their shells shut. Why do they do this?

CRUSTACEANS

Crustaceans range from mighty spider crabs to tiny shrimps. Most of these invertebrates have a body coated in a tough exoskeleton. Crustaceans' bodies are made up of many segments that are joined together.

An **exoskeleton** is a hard, flexible body covering. It is strong enough to anchor muscles that move limbs, claws, and other body parts.

A lobster is a crustacean that has ten legs, strong claws, and eyes on stalks.

Claw

Leg

Eye

Leg

A woodlouse has 14 legs and mostly eats pieces of dead plants.

Crustaceans have many legs. Some have strong claws on their front legs, to pick up food and defend themselves. They use their other legs to scuttle over rocks, or to swim. Barnacles are unusual crustaceans that are welded to rocks. They waggle their legs to catch food from the water. Crustaceans live mostly in water, but some, such as pill bugs and woodlice, live in damp places on land.

INSECTS AND SPIDERS

Insects and spiders are similar to crustaceans because they have an exoskeleton. However, they have many differences in structure, too. All insects have three main body segments. They have a head, which often has large eyes. They have a middle part, called a thorax, with six legs. They have an end part, called the abdomen. Insects are the only invertebrates with wings, though not all insects have wings.

A dragonfly uses its wings to fly quickly when hunting insects to eat.

Spiders have two body segments and eight legs. They never have wings. Spiders often make webs to catch prey.

Scorpions are close relatives of spiders, but they do not spin webs. Instead, they use a stinger on the end of their abdomen to kill prey.

Spiders spin webs from silk that they make inside their abdomens.

Abdomen

THINK ABOUT IT
Insects and spiders shed their old exoskeletons and grow new ones as they get bigger. What is the cause of this?

ECHINODERMS

Echinoderms include starfish, sea urchins, and sea cucumbers. These invertebrates have a spiny exoskeleton just under their skin. An echinoderm's body has five equal sections, arranged around a central point. Starfish have five arms. Urchins have five main lines of spines.

Some people call starfish sea stars because of their shape and because they are not fish.

COMPARE AND CONTRAST
What are the different adaptations that invertebrates have for moving around?

A sea urchin's spines help it move. They also defend it from attack.

Echinoderms have tubes filled with water in their bodies. These are connected to rows of tiny tube feet under their bodies. Squeezing water through the tubes makes the feet suck the ground, and moves the animals along. Many starfish are unusual because if an arm breaks or is bitten off, they can grow a new one!

Fish

Fish can be as different as eels, seahorses, and sharks. These vertebrates have gills, to breathe underwater. They use fins and a paddle-shaped tail to swim.

Sharks, skates, and rays have a skeleton made from cartilage. Your nose is made from this flexible material, too. These fish have pointed scales, like teeth, to protect their skin from damage.

The great white shark is a big, powerful fish that hunts prey such as sea lions.

Sardines are a type of bony fish.

THINK ABOUT IT
Swimming pushes water into a shark's mouth, past its gills, and out through slits on its side, so it can breathe. What effect does staying still have on sharks? Does staying still affect bony fish in the same way?

Other fish have hard, bony skeletons in their bodies. Bony fish have smooth, overlapping scales on their skin. They have flaps on the sides of their bodies, which cover their gills.

AMPHIBIANS

Frogs, toads, and salamanders are types of amphibians. These are vertebrates that have slimy, smooth skin with no scales. They live both in water and on land.

Most amphibians lay jellylike eggs in water. The young that hatch have gills, and swim around like fish. Later, they grow legs and breathe using lungs.

Newts have long bodies, tails, and short legs. They look like lizards.

Most amphibians are frogs and toads. They have large heads, short bodies, no tail, and long back legs. Many frogs have webbed toes for swimming.

▶▶ Tree frogs have sticky toes to grip branches. Many lay their eggs in water that has collected in plants, so their young can swim.

Reptiles

Reptiles are vertebrates with dry, scaly skin. Reptiles including lizards, snakes, turtles, alligators, and crocodiles. They breathe using lungs. Most reptiles lay eggs. Certain snakes and lizards give birth to live young.

Lizards include iguanas and geckos. They have long tails and overlapping scales. Crocodiles, alligators, and caimans are like lizards, but they have thick scales and at least 60 teeth.

⏩ **Chameleons have skin that can change color to match their surroundings!**

COMPARE AND CONTRAST
How different snakes catch food? What is the difference between snakes that use venom to kill and snakes that crush prey?

Reptiles with shells covering their backbone include turtles, which live mostly in water, and tortoises, which live on land.

Snakes are legless reptiles with no eyelids. They range in size from enormous anacondas to tiny threadsnakes.

Some snakes, such as cobras, have sharp fangs. They make venom, to kill prey before swallowing it.

Birds

Birds are as different as swans, owls, and sparrows. All birds have wings, feathers, and a light skeleton. These are adaptations for flight. Some birds, such as penguins, have wings, but cannot fly. They use their wings to swim. All birds are vertebrates.

Wings are special long, front limbs with a large area to lift a bird up in the air.

A pelican's beak is long, with a large throat pouch to scoop up fish to eat.

Pouch

Different types of birds have different beaks, which are adapted to the food they eat. For example, a hawk's bill can rip apart prey.

Birds have different feet, too. Some have claws and curved toes to perch on branches. Others have webbed feet to paddle along.

Mammals

We are mammals! Mammals are vertebrates with hair or fur on their bodies. This keeps them warm and dry. Fur can have other uses, too. For example, a cat uses its furry whiskers to sense things around it.

Female mammals feed their young on milk from their bodies. Baby mammals usually develop inside their mothers' bodies, but kangaroos have pouches on their fronts in which the baby, called a joey, develops.

A baby mammal's first food after birth is usually its mother's milk. This helps the baby grow and stay healthy.

All mammals breathe using lungs. Dolphins have to come to the surface to get air.

COMPARE AND CONTRAST
Think about the different teeth in mammals such as rats, horses, and lions. How are they adapted for eating different foods?

Mammals are adapted for living in different places. Whales and dolphins have smooth bodies, broad tails, and flippers to swim underwater. Gibbons have long arms to swing through trees. Bats have long webbed fingers to help them fly.

CLASSIFICATION

Animals are sorted into groups to make it easier to understand their similarities and differences. This is called classification. We classify animals partly based on structures, such as wings. We also classify by how animals behave, such as if they lay eggs.

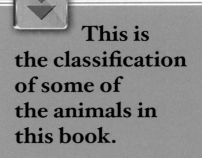

This is the classification of some of the animals in this book.

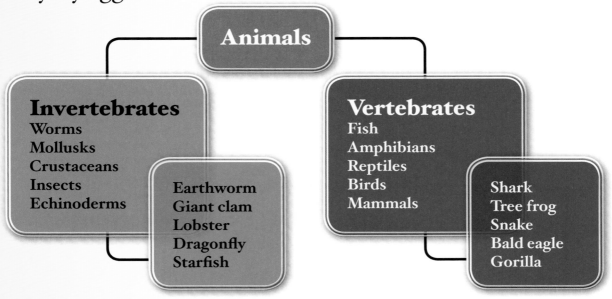

Animals

Invertebrates
Worms
Mollusks
Crustaceans
Insects
Echinoderms

Earthworm
Giant clam
Lobster
Dragonfly
Starfish

Vertebrates
Fish
Amphibians
Reptiles
Birds
Mammals

Shark
Tree frog
Snake
Bald eagle
Gorilla

A platypus is an unusual mammal. It lays eggs, and has a beak and webbed feet, like a duck.

Some animals are difficult to classify. Horseshoe crabs look like crabs, but are more closely related to scorpions. The giant panda is classified as a carnivore, or meat-eating mammal. Based on its appearance, it is related to bears. Yet, its skeleton is unlike that of other bears, and it eats only bamboo!

CHANGING STRUCTURES

Most animals have different structures depending on whether they are male or female. Male peacocks have colorful tails, but females are brown. Ants live in groups in which there are three different types of ant. Queen ants have large abdomens, to lay eggs. Workers are small and care for the group. Soldiers defend the nest.

▶▶ **Soldier ants have strong jaws to protect their nests.**

Jaw

Animals can also have different structures because of changes in nature. Snowshoe hares are brown in summer, but grow white fur in winter. This helps them hide against the snow from animals that hunt them.

Sometimes people make changes that affect animals. When rivers and ponds are polluted, frogs can get sick and even grow extra legs.

Soil, air, and water are **polluted** when they are made dirty or harmful by something else.

Coral turn white and get sick when the seawater in which they live becomes too warm.

GLOSSARY

abdomen The end body section of animals such as insects and crustaceans.

adaptations Special features or ways of behaving that help a living thing survive.

amphibians Vertebrate animals that lay eggs in water. Their young breathe with gills. When they are adults, they live on land and breathe through lungs.

backbone A stiff rod or bone in the back of vertebrates.

caiman Any of several Central and South American reptiles closely related to and looking like alligators.

cartilage A tough, flexible material supporting the body of some fish. Cartilage is also found in other animals.

classification The process of sorting something into groups.

crustaceans Invertebrate animals that have a hard shell and segmented body. They live mostly in water.

echinoderms Invertebrate animals that have a spiny exoskeleton and five equal sections arranged around a central point. They live mostly in the sea.

fangs Long, sharp teeth.

gills Body parts used to breathe underwater.

guts The stomach and intestines inside animals.

invertebrates Animals without backbones.

limbs Legs or arms.

mollusks Invertebrate animals with hard shells and soft bodies.

prey Animals hunted for food.

related Part of the same family.

scales Small, tough plates covering and protecting skin in fish and reptiles.

tentacles Thin, flexible body parts often on an animal's head. They are used to grasp, move around, or feed with.

thorax The middle section of an insect's body, with legs, and sometimes wings, attached.

tide The daily rise and fall of the sea.

venom Poison made by animals.

vertebrates Animals with backbones.

webbed Skin stretched between fingers or toes.

FOR MORE INFORMATION

Books

Burnie, David. *Kingfisher Animal Encyclopedia*. London, UK: Kingfisher, 2011.

Rand, Casey. *Classification of Animals* (Sci-Hi: Life Science). North Mankato, MN: Raintree, 2009.

Siwanowicz, Igor. *Animals Up Close*. New York, NY: DK Publishing, 2009.

Spelman, Lucy. *National Geographic Animal Encyclopedia: 2,500 Animals with Photos, Maps, and More!* Washington, D.C.: National Geographic Children's Books, 2012.

Super Nature Encyclopedia. New York, NY: DK Children, 2012.

Websites

Due to the changing nature of Internet links, Rosen Publishing has developed an online list of Websites related to the subject of this book. This site is updated regularly. Please use this link to access the list:

http://www.rosenlinks.com/lfo/anim

INDEX